VAN GOGH IN BRIXTON

VAN GOGH IN BRIXTON

SHAUN TRAYNOR

**M
P**

MUSWELL PRESS LTD

First published in Great Britain October 2013
by Muswell Press Ltd
6 Pinchin Street
London E1 1SA

Photo of Van Gogh House © Elaine Kramer

Many of these poems have been published in magazines and periodicals,
principally in the *London Magazine*, *The Author*, *English Pen*, *Agenda* and
Aquarius.

The Author wishes to express his gratitude to Carol Hughes for permission
to use an extract from a letter from Ted Hughes and to Sebastian Barker for
permission to use an extract from one of his letters.

A CIP record for this book is available from the British Library

ISBN 978-0-9575568-2-9

Text and Cover Design by Bewick Abel Thompson

Printed and Bound by Shortrun Press Ltd
Sowton Industrial Estate
Bittern Road
Exeter 7LW EX2

www.muswell-press.co.uk

FOR
URSULA

BY THE SAME AUTHOR

POETRY COLLECTIONS

THE HARDENING GROUND
IMAGES IN WINTER
SHAKESPEARE'S LAST DRINK (AS PAMPHLET)

FOR CHILDREN

NOVELS
HUGO O'HUGE, THE CHILDREN'S GIANT
THE GIANTS' OLYMPICS
A LITTLE MAN IN ENGLAND
THE LOST CITY OF BELFAST

AS EDITOR
THE POOLBEG BOOK OF IRISH POETRY FOR CHILDREN

CONTENTS

POET'S INTRODUCTION

These poems have been written over a number of years and in different parts of England and Ireland. They have been arranged chronologically and by place.
I hope they form a narrative and are intended to be a sequel to my last collection, *Images in Winter*.

THE OIL SLICK

I am the oiled bird,
caught in a spillage,
being cleaned by kind hands.

Better now,
I am set upon a widening ocean,

but am wary and still
when strange ships pass in the night.

WITHOUT HURT, THE WRITER'S ROOM

They have come to sleep in my study
I have boxed up my books,
brought in an extra bed,
put the cover on my desk-top.
I have pinned up their "last-visit" pictures
to make them feel at home.

They are still at arm's length.

Then suddenly it is a noisy, happy, children's room
where toys get broken
and I mend them.

Time is in a capsule.

Then it's Sunday
and back to their mother's
as I return to the forget-me-nots:

a scarf without a neck,
a slipper without a foot;

I recite the lines of practicality,
out of sight, out of mind...
and act upon it.

Only through clichés,
by leaning on the common experience,
can I re-enter that nerveless paradise, the writer's room,
become a medium, thin as smoke,
through which eternity must pass...

knowing somewhere far away,
a woman kneels but cannot pray;
knowing somewhere far away,
a woman kneels to button up my children's day.

FROM A WILTSHIRE WINDOW

The sky wets and blackens itself,
winter comes.

The last rose bush beats against the window,
its dark leaves falling.

The trees across the road are like dancers,
their naked arms and trunks up-stretched, swaying
and whipping in the wind.

Convulsive,

again and again, the rose stalk beats the pane
as my trembling, disturbed mind
throws crockery across the room.

THE WAITRESS

She moves from table to table, stooping,
her job's yoke on the small
of her small back.

Men exchange remarks with her
and she smiles.
She makes no rendezvous.

Outside her starry flat
house-martins build:
their wing-flap, like a musical tapestry,
lingers above the city

whilst in bed,
men's words twine like ivy in her hair.

HILL WALK

If I lived in a bigger house I would write better poems,
I would find a room for every mood and looking out
find different kinds of solace.

Tonight for example,
I wanted to write about the hill sequence
where Ursula and I had walked today
and in our walking, as well as holding hands,
we had opened, for the first time this year,
our windowed minds to Nature:

but coming back here
there were the chores to do,
the cooking and the washing up,
the lighting of a fire -
even the logs had to be halved
to fit into the tiny grate -

So we sit, half-bemused by dusk,
ignorant of television,
knowing the lark is still singing valiantly,
and we remember, we recall
the redbreast, beloved redbreast, our winter's ally,
like ourselves, bemused that today
so much was going on -

for today came the wren, today came the partridge,
and as if to make a metaphor of our senses,
a few landed water-hens, running in their silly way -

Coming upstairs then to write this poem
in the half-light of a dewy April evening.
I see the hawthorn tree next door has burst into flower -
there is no doubt my step upon the stair
follows its ascension. I am triumphant
on the lintel step-in of my study…

Yet coming into this narrow, fusty room
I must keep in my memory's eye
the broad expanse of where we walked today;
how we rose above birdsong,
saw to the south, Westbury,
to the north, the beginnings of Swindon.

There was no compression.

Yet to type these words,
I have to call into this tiny, high-windowed room
a long walk along the world's ridges -
and where is Ursula?

The poem designed to be about a unity,
in its creation, divides.

Next door a man bickers with his wife,
she with her child,
there seems no point -

except perhaps not to lose
a feeling of what happened this early afternoon, a memory -
not of the sky, nor of the great descending hills,
nor tiny wren -

but of how we felt, majestic, free
and a part of an undying possibility.

FROM GLASTONBURY

By Woodward Way there is a tree
that is as strange as strange can be,
it bursts its flower bright in May,
then again on Christmas Day.

A cutting from the Holy Thorn,
to mark the day when Christ was born,
was brought by farmers long ago
and set to see if it would grow.

From Wearyall and famous Tor,
where Joseph's staff did twig and flower,
it came to Cannings where we breathe
the scent of sweet Gethsemene.

It says that Christ in England stood
on the lands of Gwyn ap Nudd,
whatever truth that there may be,
is in the flowering of this tree.

All Cannings, Wiltshire.

WRITER IN RESIDENCE

Today I climbed Cannings Cross
and a few other hills beyond;

at half past four I was over Patney roadside
investigating two quails mating in a hedgerow;

at five o'clock reports had me
on the main Marlborough to Pewsey highroad,
gazing up.

Many cars passed between four and six,
I skipped up on the ditch to give them room -

help them speed -

but some drivers stopped, asked me what I was doing,

"Looking for inspiration?"

One driver was more persistent, he said,

"I mean, what do you do out here, all day, Shaun?"

I said - and my brow furrowed with the effort of replying -

(It's not a question I would ever ask myself)

"I'm trying to forge a new language
which might, one day, be called the language of the sky."

At half past five I was back near 'Cannings'
counting the cows (the heavy milk-train)
out of John Hues' farm.

At a quarter to six I was spotted
(so they told me later)
in the big field that goes to make up Tan Hill.

At five to six,
Reg-the-Wall-Builder took me home;
I sat with the gang in the back of the van,
"Did you have a good day ?" they asked.
"What were you doing today?" they asked.

"Just keeping an eye on things for you."

I replied.

JUDGING A POETRY COMPETITION

Judging a poetry competition is the opposite
of having your flat broken into,
your pockets rifled,
your Barclay-card mis-used,
letters from an "ex"
being scanned for some contemporary reference.

Now I
am the peeping-tom,
the sneak-thief person,
who steams open envelopes,
leaves them without body-prints -
P.C. POET

"Are you the heavy breather, Madam/Sir ?
You have one minute to tell me what makes you tick.

Manuscripts become a jammed
call centre switchboard
and I am saying,
"Wrong number, Wrong number!"
Listen to my laughter ringing,
like the clatter of a rejected coin.

Then there comes

THE POEM

about a lover who has lost, about where love
has been through the intensive-care system –
failed or was failed…

the poem's artefact is like frosted glass,
a hospital screen, yet behind it
drips someone's tears.

THIS IS THE WINNER

I say,
written by a loser.

Who cares ?

THE EXHIBITION

Reading a poem in the library
to an audience as unsullied as an un-thumbed book,
I remember a spinster friend of mine once saying,
"I hate being a book that is never looked at,
never torn, never read, never fingered through;
not to be ear-marked, sullied, is a sin."

I consider how I must appear
as I read my poem about the moon above Stonehenge,
when the moon is naked and I wonder at the clothes I wear,
 the respectable clothes;

I have become my audience.

I read somewhere, "All poets are mad,"
and round the library walls are paintings
from patients at the local Mental Institution,
pictures of planets, sun-coloured by the frailty
of the artists' minds.

When I write poems,
they come to me from that part of me which is frail,
life-marked, down-at-heel, wine-bottled, fag-end-crushed;
yet I have no appearance of it,
now.

Suddenly, I hear the artists coming:

behind the glass of the library's high, locked doors,
a mob is gathering; noses
 pressed against glass, eyes like shell-fish -
look at the baggy trousers, the shoes on the wrong feet...
They clamour for me to finish, for the reading to end.
It is their turn...

I finish with a poem about identity,
about waking anxious in the night,
about wanting so desperately to get things right.
Then the doors are opened and the sleep-walkers come
to gaze at their pictures of a Van Gogh sun -

and I mingle.

WRITER IN SCHOOL

Saying goodbye, getting my cheque,
I remember the clown,
who in my childhood passed
from town to town,
making the children laugh -
and fattened on their laughter,
made a run for it.

I remember how
in the darkness of a cloakroom, I
being last to leave,
saw him fingering our parents' thruppeny bits which
we had, as children, tossed with such careless mirth
into his cap.

Later,
I saw him at the bus-stop, cap-in-hand,
counting each piece of our pleasure,
turning us into coins.

RECOLLECTIONS AND INTIMATIONS

In the storm we lit oil-lamps
and a century fell away.

In the shadows flickering from the crumbled wick
images passed, like ghosts long forgotten:

a farmyard at dusk, a tall man moving,
cloaked, heavy-booted, lantern aloft -
my grandfather;

On the wall, his portrait,
suddenly alight, then darkening;
paint glistening in its own renaissance,

then another - my mother's uncle,
a schools' inspector.

Then direct from childhood,
heard again in the country silence of this Wiltshire moor,
the click of old Ulster door-latches;

outside the movement of cattle,
the muffled banging of their sides against a barn,
as in a dream.

It is bedtime
and with my lamp, I climb the stairs:
in the stairs' mirror I can see a flame reflected,
an image held, where I am old,
old as my ancestors, someone else's recollection;

within that tiny flame
I know myself,
and quickly blow it out.

EGGSHELL

(for Sydney Vale and in his memory)

From his hide the artist,
hunched, attentive,
keeps a watch on subtleties:

the garden is embraced by twilight,
it shudders, then turns -

surprisingly,
there is still a touch of pink in the flower-bed,
more predictably, some darkening mauve across Box Hill.

Then suddenly a little touch of chlorophyll stands out, brim-
ming, immaculately still;
it is this fragile, eggshell-cup of colour,
the artist knows he mustn't spill.

Mount Pleasant Artists' Retreat, Reigate

THE ARTIST'S WIFE

(for Bob and Morna)

Crouched by the door she listens
even to a brush-stroke.
"Is it now you want your tea?"

The great man comes out,
his mind a-gape with landscapes
of the imagination.

She serves him,
her belly full with child:

anxiously
they eye each other,
break bread,
eat the evening meal.

Carrowholly

SECOND MARRIAGE

The quarry lies empty now,
like an old dog's skull;
the house, its predator,
stands grey and shining,
daily painted by rain and silver sun.

The rainbow hues of evening
light the entire valley
and we are happy now,
smoke rising from one chimney.

We also keep one door closed.

Westport

DANDY

(for Charles Humanu and in his memory)

I cannot believe you are dead, dear boy,
my goodness, how I miss you;
every time I come here, this place
is about you walking up and down the stairs
in a rather splendid smoking jacket;

yes, you were vain
but not without cause.
It is now your kindness that I want to record:
how when my back was bad
you stripped me, massaged me,
gave me financial advice;
under your fists, made me repeat,

"I will shore up money against old age."

They say that you stumbled and fell
in an English street, died in England,
yet your internationalism demanded
an unmarked grave and,
as I believe, a request for secrecy –

"Let no man know."

I hope we meet some time;
snooker in the evening
is not the same without you,
nor is toast in the morning.

By the way, I'm wearing the black shoes, sorry,
the brown shoes
(I always got that wrong didn't I ?)
with the green cords you recommended…

Mount Pleasant Artists' Retreat, Reigate.

GROWING OLD

First it's your friends, making it.

They sink their savings into a cul-de-sac,
ask you up for dinner,
and you know you're going to sit
in yet another Parker-Knoll,
sipping malt whiskey
until it all becomes quite painless
except your brain is growing greyer, cold and old.

I remember when we used to meet in pubs,
we stood from half-past-five 'til closing time,
then adjourned to a Greek restaurant,
where we broke plates, cashed cheques,
and none of us owned anything -

least of all our wives.

Now it's like going back to Ireland,
my friends have become my parents,
neat houses, large spare rooms,
on the wall Babe Rainbow instead of flying ducks,
and setting it all off, a piece of crappy sculpture -
"made by a friend, you know,"
instead of the delf, Alsatian dog,
that sat on all our native window-sills.

I tell them narrative poems
about life in the raw,
they say, "You are a one!"
and "How is she?" and "She?
Still on the loose?" they say salaciously,
polishing their chains.

I worry that I'm becoming unbecoming:

I kept it up all last year,
until one of these best friends, old buddies, said,
"I feel I've been here for such a long time - on earth, I mean -
and, to be honest, Shaun, so much accomplished, so much
done."

Then I knew it was time to run.

THE CANCERED TREE

The tree outside the library window
was always skinny, bedraggled, too cloistered
from the sun, too close to buildings;

but this Autumn as we watched,
we saw first the nicotine-stained finger of a single leaf,
then, within days, the whole tree was stained,
its lungs finished.

In the winds of November
it tossed and bowed and was sick;
all its leaves fell off,
the rain pelted it, its naked trunk.

In the Spring instead of growing again,
it took the blight. A man from the council came
with a machine on expanding legs, inspected it…

then starting from the top, demolished it:
first the brain, then the body's trunk,
then the very roots.
Then he raked about in the soil afterwards
in case there was any trace of life there, left behind.

They took all of it away in a lorry.
Maybe now it's a book; this one.

For myself, when I am finally casting about,
knowing that there will be no green shoots of hope
and when the pain sets in,
I doubt if I will be so philosophic -
more likely I'll be crying, weeping all the time,
like the rain in Lancashire, that lashes at this window

where a tree used to stand.

Upholland School, Wigan.

RINGING THE BELL FOR THE LAST TIME

I let the long, rusty tongue of the old bell toll out, lap
its final message.
I felt my own tongue going dry
and it hurt to swallow;
my glands seemed to be swelling up.

I watched the children come running to line,
all dressed in national costume,
party day - end of term,

they looked beautiful.

Then it was assembly
and I had rehearsed a speech,
something along the lines of

*"Thank-you for turning the twilight of my years
into a glorious sunset..."*

something like that.

But I was not, in fact,
called upon to speak.

There was, I admit,
a reference
to my leaving:

in the new (acting) head-mistress's speech,
she gave a very full address to *"the problems of discipline
we might all face if we don't all pull together;"*

and

"If certain short and long-term practices aren't put in place…"
something bad would happen.

She talked a lot about punctuality
and about *a general tightening up of…*
well, just about everything.

Then she talked about *getting rid of old, dead-wood ideas*
and it was at that point that she mentioned me…
well nearly:

*"Mr aghm, aghm…is leaving us.
We all wish him, Mr aghm -
all the best."*

That was it.
I was so glad I had taken my wife's advice
not to wear a suit.

At half past three I slipped away,
like the white-haired master in Yevtushenko's famous poem
about a schoolmaster slipping away -

he moves without defences…
worn out… snow falling on him…
he whitens to white…

It was the nearest I ever got to Art.

WHOSE SIDE ARE THE COWS ON ANYWAY?

A landmine and a workman's hut,
cows grazing lazily in the tranquility of Tyrone,
a trigger-wire amongst the rushes, a landmine
and an army patrol on guard
down the road to Dungannon:

A cow meanders to the trigger wire,
an assassin wipes sweat off his stop-watch,
the cow nibbles the life-line,
a soldier dreams of England -
the assassin activates the device,
a cloud drifts in the gathering wind,
the cow swishes its tail,
midges gyrate in irritation.

THE PHOENIX

There is a peace in this city, a holy incense
of aftermath and ashes,
smoke from bombs and the dying of a siren.

There is a silence, respectful
amongst this newly created dereliction;
there is a sanctity amidst the limbs and skulls.

It is arid;
this is peace-time, war's ghost.

I watch a child, half-schooled, scrawl on a wall
this city's latest wit-graffiti -

DEATH TO THE FENIX

it is, you'll find, a tricky bird to burn.

RETURN TO THE CITY

Driven again,
we return to the city
we know as not "user-friendly."
but a city of like minds -
each one of us nursing - as in an underclass - a talent
for which the art-form has not, as yet, been invented; defined.

So we eschew
the rural supper-safari where one must explain one's self,
we eschew the concept of "friends by environment,"
the country,
we eschew the trophy cabinet for the cardboard box,
 maybe…

but we live now in a place of choice where one need not speak,
explain.

AN AEROPLANE OVER CLAPHAM COMMON

1.

It was the bluest sky of any summer,
defying artistry,
until a pilot
in a machine, stronger than the heart,
traced a straight line of chalk
across the vacuum blue,
turned and drew -
sistine-chapelled -
another pristine universe.

2.

Later,
I saw a broken kite hanging on a tree
and in The Windmill,
a woman in a flying jacket
buying pints
and laughing with her friends.

VAN GOGH IN BRIXTON

In Hackford Road, SW9,
there is a house
where Van Gogh
lived,
fell in love…

there is of course,
the obligatory blue plaque,
but more importantly
the woman who lives there
has placed a vase of dried sunflowers
in the window:

a nice touch that -

the blue plaque,
the sunflowers,
a little bit of green
attracting sunlight into a city garden,

yet across the road
at the school where I teach,

there is a bunker

where the school keeper
keeps coal.

Note:
It was some time after this short, seemingly happy, sojourn in Hackford Road that the young Vincent set off for the Flemish coal-mines, to one of the unhappiest periods of his life.

VAUXHALL CROSS

I must somehow attempt, attempt
to make permanent what I witnessed today;

a battered van stopped at the lights,

(I was in my own car, battered, in five lanes of overheating,
stationary traffic)

I glanced across and saw two workmen,

their vehicle indicated they were SOUTH WEST PLUMBERS -
a driver and his companion;

I saw them suddenly
slump back in their seats,
their heads lolling back, as if their necks were broken,
like battery hens at the end of their working life,
they lay like overall-ed corpses, laid out, mummified,
completely knackered by work.

I suppose the Tories who had set the scene
and New Labour who gratefully accepted it,
could take succour from this vignette -
men in work, exhausted by work
and the backdrop, the glorious backdrop -
the new MI6 building rising like an empire,

and so many new offices and luxury flats, hundreds of them,
all piled on one on top of another
like cars in a car dump, jangled
and everywhere

evidence

of real urban regeneration.

Here is the perfect free-fall, kaleidoscope, hold-me-forever image
held most dear by politicians,
cranes and building machinery, roads up,
loads of noise, a cacophony of activity,
and all of this

where Handel once composed.

And the hundreds of cars, organized at the lights, regimented
like a Nuremburg rally, criss-crossing at the seven crossings of Vaux-
hall Cross,
 all in perfect formation, aka Leni Riefenstahl,

as the sun hits the polluted river like a spray of spent New Cov-
ent Garden violets.

Then the lights changed

and the plumbers were lost forever...

Except that they began to haunt my mind:
where had I seen heads like that before?

Then I remembered, pictures from Easter Island,
The *moai*, their great heads hewn out of rock,
staring out at nothing.

RUIN

(For Ursula)

The geraniums you potted on our window sill
have now become a flowering album of our travels,
we saw them everywhere, do you remember,
in so many different countries,
suddenly lighting up a landscape,

or making a quite ordinary courtyard
force us both to catch our breath?

In them also resides a dream,

that one day you and I might buy a ruin,
do it up, and in its courtyard, plant
a hundred of such red geraniums,
that so in time,

two younger lovers will walk by,
kiss and murmur in our courtyard,
say "how happy must the people be
who live behind the flowers."

You will come out, startled
by this impertinent intrusion;

then I will remind you
of how we used to talk about people like us,

 so many years ago.

60 Meadow Road sw8

RE-VISITING A RESTAURANT I ONCE KNEW

(for Martin)

Sat there today, place empty,
lunchtime: food cold,
decorations kitch,
kitch as in the old Belfast joke about flares,
"Don't worry, the style will come round again."

There was a time…

when the food came piping hot, braised
as we were, bouncing off a hot plate of dreams,
every table full
of cries of

Kleftiko!
Dolmades!
With chips!
Retzina!

Café Hellenic…
Metaxa!

A time - believe me -
when the *Gents* was full of young men pissing rainbows

and the swing door of the *Ladies*, swung with hips and youth.

Today emptiness –
from Toulouse-Lautrec to Van Gogh,
(just the chair)
from burlesque to pathos,
finally
to Edward Hopper.

It is the empty chair, the chairs, the empty tables, that pose the
problem;
empty spaces in a bar or restaurant, spaces
which once were filled anywhere and everywhere....

the terror of the now consumes me,
what to do when the world is empty
of all we know and love?

Universally flit

from town to country, country to continent,
learn a different language, find a new way
to walk back home?

CODA

WHY I WRITE CHILDREN'S STORIES

(After the painting, *The Doctor*, by Sir Henry Fildes)

When the great man's child died
on Christmas day,

he reincarnated in his studio
a make-believe, labourer's cottage;

arranged to have the sun shine each day
at a certain angle, appropriately
to light the curls on the forehead of a placed child
lying there, recovering
after treatment under a doctor's kind hand…

So with my children's stories,
I recreate the events which only poetry
can properly describe.

REVIEWS OF PREVIOUS WORK

THE HARDENING GROUND

In this his first collection Shaun Traynor takes his place amongst his peers from the North of Ireland and the South. His dramatic Meditations on the Suspension of Stormont deserves its place in the canon.
(Desmond O'Grady, Hibernia Review of Books)
The last poem in the book, the magnificent Mediations on the Suspension of Stormont, changed my thinking about Ireland.
(Mary Hardy, Irish Post)
Strongest are the more formal pieces like The Child and the Thrush where the influence of Patrick Kavanagh is for once happy.
(Edna Longley, The Irish Times)
His poetry is open, direct, unedged, his feelings immediately and clearly rendered, his dictions and rhythms simple to a point of an attractive naiveté.
(Terry Eagleton, The Tablet)
Love is this young man's concern, but he is also aware of the harsher necessities as in A Labourer's Lament.
(John Montague, The Times Literary Supplement)

IMAGES IN WINTER

There are several new notes in this second book which bode well for Shaun Traynor's future work. All the signs of maturity are here.
The rhythms are stronger, the images have a more telling precision, his romanticism is more controlled.
(Shirley Toulson, The Ulster Tatler)

Shaun Traynor's new book is a delight, the writing is fresh and exact, he is in touch with the old spring, the old jauntiness of language, its resilience, its lasting singing power. His poetry is an act of faith, his rhythms a gift of grace. Traynor takes chances, there is a sense of risk in his poetry, a sense that this business of writing poetry actually matters.
(Robert Welch, Literary Review)

I enjoyed every poem — especially Soyland, Affirmation, Journey to Work, The Rooks Song, Long Walks towards Pubs, The Magician, The Joke, Failing, Wedding Anniversary (a marvellous little poem!) Nocturne, Isle of Dogs, Maureen's Cat, In Ireland Once …
(From a letter from Ted Hughes)

WRITING FOR CHILDREN

Shaun Traynor's writing for children exudes love and tenderness towards children and their earth. His modern fairytales with their contemporary settings capture children's imagination from the beginning.
(Irish Children's Book Trust Guide to Children's Books.)

THE POOLBEG BOOK OF IRISH POETRY FOR CHIL-
DREN *… is a very attractive anthology with its roots firmly in Ireland but its appeal stretching far beyond.*
(Julia Eccleshare, The Guardian)